Fun Reptile Facts for Kids 9 - 12

Fun Animal Facts for Kids Book 4

Jacquelyn Elnor Johnson

www.CrimsonHillBooks.com

First edition, October 2016.
Revised edition, January 2021.

Cataloguing in Publication Data

Johnson, Jacquelyn Elnor

Fun Reptile Facts for Kids 9-12

Description: Crimson Hill Books trade hardcover edition | Nova Scotia, Canada

ISBN: 978-1-988650-88-3 (Hardcover – Ingram)

BISAC: JNF003170 Juvenile Nonfiction: Animals – Pets
JNF051150 Juvenile Nonfiction: Science & Nature - Zoology
JNF003190 Juvenile Nonfiction: Animals - Reptiles & Amphibians

THEMA: PSVF - Zoology: amphibians & reptiles (herpetology)
WNGS - Reptiles & amphibians as pets
YNNM - Children's / Teenage general interest: Reptiles & amphibians

Record available at https://www.bac-lac.gc.ca/eng/Pages/home.aspx

Book design: Jesse Johnson

Crimson Hill Books
(a division of)
Crimson Hill Products Inc.
Wolfville, Nova Scotia
Canada

Crimson Hill
Books

This colourful wild iguana is basking on a rock.
Basking means warming up your body in the sunlight.
Or, for pet lizards, under a heat lamp.

This is another kind of wild iguana.

Have you ever seen this guy?

Have you ever seen a strange-looking creature like this guy? Maybe at a zoo? Or when you were on vacation?

If not, but I showed you a picture of just their face, would you guess that this is a fish?

Though it does have a fishy-looking face, one way you can tell that this animal is not a fish is there are eyelids. That's something fish don't have.

And there are some other clues that this creature lives on land.

Can you spot them?

One is that it has nostrils. Nostrils are nose openings. This means it breathes air, just like people do.

Although this animal has scales, its skin is dry and cool, not wet and slippery like a fish's skin.

It has a triangle-shaped head. That's another important clue that tells you it must be either a snake or a lizard.

This wildly colourful creature is an iguana. Their name sounds like this: eee-gwaugh-naa. Iguanas are one type of lizard.

All lizards are reptiles.

Reptiles are a very large group of creatures. They're among the oldest and oddest creatures on earth! They come in almost every size and colour you can imagine. And they have some astonishing superpowers! That's what this book is about.

Some reptiles can swim. Others run, crawl, slither or fly.

Though we have lived in their world, and they have lived in our world, for many thousands of years, there are still many mysteries about these fascinating creatures to discover.

Perhaps you'll become an animal explorer and help answer some of the questions people still have about reptiles!

What are reptiles?

Reptiles are the large group of animals that have scales.

Almost all reptiles except some sea snakes lay their eggs on land.

The reptile family is huge! It includes:

- turtles and tortoises
- lizards and snakes
- crocodiles, alligators and caimans
- birds
- taratua

Some reptiles have two legs. Some have four legs. Some seem to have no legs at all.

No reptile has hair or fur, but some have feathers.

Their name, *reptile*, comes from a word that means "to creep." But many reptiles don't creep. Instead, they crawl, leap, climb, run, walk, swim, dive, slither, glide or fly.

Reptiles live on every continent on earth except Antarctica, though most wild reptiles live in tropical places.

All reptiles have cool, dry skin.

Some of their skin is covered in scales. Scales are made from a body substance called *keratin.* Say it like this: care-a-tin. Keratin is the same substance that your fingernails and toenails are made from.

That's one way reptiles are like people.

This is a chameleon sitting in a rubber tree.

What other ways are reptiles like people?

All people have lungs to hold the air they breathe into their bodies. So do all reptiles, even the ones that live most of their lives in the water, like sea snakes.

Both reptiles and people have bodies covered with skin.

The two important things both reptiles and humans have inside their bodies are their brains and their boney skeletons.

All the bones in your body connect to form your skeleton. If you had no skeleton, you would be a blobby shape, like a jelly-fish. If you had no skeleton, you couldn't sit up, stand, walk or run.

Both people and reptiles are *vertebrates.* Here's how to say it: ver-teh-bray-ts. All vertebrates have a bony skull in their head with a brain inside the skull.

All vertebrates have a skeleton. As part of their skeletons, they all have a spinal cord or a backbone, or both.

If you don't know where your backbone is, here's how to find it. Put your hand at the centre of your back. You'll feel a hard bone there. Now, put your hand at the top of your back, just under your neck. There's a hard bone there, too.

Both times, you have touched your backbone, near the bottom and near the top. A backbone is made up of many small connecting bones. These bones are called vertebrae.

Mammals, birds, reptiles, amphibians and fish are all vertebrates. They all have a skeleton with a backbone.

Even turtles, that have a hard shell, have a backbone and a skeleton.

These are freshwater alligators.

How are reptiles different from people and other mammals?

Almost all reptiles lay eggs. They do not have live babies.

All mammals have live babies except for the platypus of Australia, a very strange mammal that lays eggs. Mammals are animals with four legs, lungs, hair or fur and a backbone. Horses, bears, lions, dogs, cats, elephants, whales and people are all mammals.

Most reptile parents do not care for their babies. Instead, they lay their eggs and leave before the eggs hatch. Some birds and almost all mammals are good parents, looking after their babies until they are adults. These good animal parents teach their children how to find food and survive on their own.

All mammals can hear. Some reptiles can't hear well or can't hear at all. Snakes and turtles have no outer ear. They hear mostly by vibrations in the earth, not sounds.

Lizards do have an outer ear, but you might have to look closely to be able to see it. Also, very strangely, some lizards have a hole right through their heads. If you have a pet leopard gecko you can hold them up and see straight through their brain! No one knows why they have this. It's just one of the strange secrets of the reptile world!

Crocodiles and alligators have good hearing! They probably developed this because they need it to hunt for their food, or avoid their enemies.

Mammals are warm-blooded. Their bodies can warm up or cool down when they need to.

All reptiles except birds are cold-blooded. This means they rely on the sun to get warm. They must find a cool place in the shade when they need to cool off. They have no way to warm themselves by turning their food into warmth. This is something mammals can do. Reptiles have waterproof skin, something only a very few mammals have. One of the mammals that is waterproof is the chinchilla. Seals are another.

Here is something else reptiles can do, but people can't. They have muscles inside their eyes that allow them to make their eyes take in more light, or less light. Because they can do this, they can see much better in low light than humans can! Low light is early in the morning, evening and on very cloudy days.

This is a green basilisk lizard, also called a water-walker. When frightened or escaping from prey, the water-walker really can run across the top of the water!

Are reptiles just modern dinosaurs?

People didn't live in the time of the dinosaurs, but some reptiles and very small mammals did. Reptiles developed before the dinosaurs! This makes reptiles the longest-living and most ancient species of creatures on earth!

Reptiles first developed, scientists say, about 310 million to 320 million years ago. One way we know this is there are fossil footprints of *Hylonomus*, the earliest known reptile, in Canada. Here's how to say their name: Hi-LON-no-muss. These Hylonomus footprints were made 315 million years ago.

The earliest people didn't develop until about 100,000 years ago. This means reptiles are much more ancient that humans.

Humans have never lived in a world where there were no reptiles.

Some scientists now believe that some types of dinosaurs might have also been types of lizards.

Or, dinosaurs might have been a completely different species of creatures.

Dinosaurs have been extinct for a very long time. Extinct means every one of them died. We have only their bones, and sometimes their eggs, to give us clues about what they looked like and how they lived.

Reptiles, both in the past and the ones alive today, are quite different than dinosaurs. The shape of their bones and skeletons are different. The ways their bodies work are different.

Reptiles' legs usually come out from the sides of their bodies. Birds are the only reptiles that have legs under their bodies.

Dinosaurs' legs were more like modern birds and mammals, coming out under their bodies, allowing them to walk and run.

If our legs came out from the sides of our bodies, we would only be able to move slowly on land, as reptiles do.

Creatures alive today that may be the closest to being like ancient dinosaurs are crocodiles and birds.

This grass snake is tasting the air. Photo by Wikimages via Pixabay.

Are reptiles the same as amphibians?

Amphibians are another family of creatures that is different from both reptiles and mammals. Some of the amphibians you have probably seen are frogs, toads and salamanders. Newts are also amphibians.

Reptiles have scales, and some have feathers, but amphibians don't. Amphibians spend most of their lives in or near water. They need to keep their skin moist. They lay their eggs in water.

Amphibians' eggs have a soft shell. Reptile eggs have a hard shell, like chicken eggs.

Amphibians don't have claws. Reptiles do.

Amphibians can absorb water through their skin. Most reptiles can't.

This turtle is a type of reptile.

How many types of reptiles are there?

There are more than 20,000 different creatures that we know of in the reptile family. There could be more that no one has ever seen.

Almost every year, scientists discover new types of bugs and other creatures. It could be there are birds or other reptiles waiting for science explorers to find!

Most reptiles we already know about are lizards, snakes or birds. Here are the number of different types (scientists call this *species*) of reptiles alive today:

- **Birds** – more than 10,000 species
- **Lizards and snakes** – more than 9,600 species
- **Turtles and tortoises** – about 400 species
- **Crocodiles, alligators and caimans** – 25 species
- **Tuatara** – just 1 species.

This is the world's largest snake, the anaconda. Though it looks ferocious, it is not the world's most dangerous snake!

What's the world's largest reptile?

The world's largest snake, the anaconda, is truly scary! The biggest one ever found was 30 feet (9 m) long and 44 inches around its body (1.1 m). Anacondas are big enough to eat dogs or adult deer!

Compared to the anaconda, the world's largest bird doesn't seem very big, though it is bigger than a human adult. This big bird is the ostrich. It can grow up to 9 feet (or 2.7 m) tall!

Big as these creatures these are, they still aren't the largest reptile. Consider the komodo dragon of Indonesia. It weighs less than the anaconda, but is still big enough to eat a goat. Or a person.

A Komodo Dragon can grow up to 11 feet (or 3.3 m) long.

This is a komodo dragon.

Not only are these guys big, they are heavy! An adult male Komodo Dragon can weigh as much as 365 pounds (166 kg).

There are sea turtles that have a shell that is 9 feet (or 2.7 m) long! If you found a shell left behind by a turtle that had died, you could turn that shell upside down and use it for a rowboat!

But that's still small compared to the largest saltwater crocodile ever found. This monster was 23 feet long (7 m) long and weighed an incredible 2,200 pounds (1,000 kg)!

This makes the Saltwater Crocodile the winner in the World's Biggest Reptile contest.

The tiny bee hummingbird is the world's smallest bird. This is a male. During breeding season, its head will turn red.

What is the world's smallest reptile?

The world's smallest bird is the tiny bee hummingbird. It is just 2 ¼ inches (5.7 centimetres) long. Yet this tiny bird can do all the amazing things every hummingbird can do. Hummingbirds are the world's only creature that can fly upside-down and backwards!

The world's smallest snake is the thread snake. It is not much wider than a piece of thread and just 4 inches (10 cm) long.

But if you travel to the Dominican Republic, you might be lucky enough to see the world's smallest

This is a bearded dragon. They can make great pets.

reptile. It's the tiny Jaragua sphaero or dwarf gecko. It's smaller than your big toe. Just a bit bigger than half an inch (17 mm) long, this tiny gecko was unknown until it was discovered in 2001.

This is a sea snake.

Some reptiles have water-tight skin

Scales on a snake's or lizard's body or a bird's legs and feet keep them dry and help that animal keep enough water in its body.

People need to drink a lot of water (or other liquids) to keep enough water in our bodies. This is because we lose a lot of water from our bodies every day, mostly by sweating to keep cool or by peeing to get waste out of our bodies.

Animals that don't need as much water can go longer without a drink. This helps them survive longer in times when there is no rain and they can't find water.

Reptiles breath air into their lungs, just like mammals do. But some reptiles can also take water into their mouth and get the oxygen directly out of the water.

Mammals must breath in air to get the oxygen we need to survive. We can't breathe water, as some reptiles can.

All reptiles have four legs

All reptiles are tetrapods. Tetrapod means a creature with four feet or legs. Amphibians, reptiles, birds and mammals are tetrapods.

But how can this be true? Many birds only have two legs. Snakes don't seem to have any legs at all!

Here's the surprising answer. When you look closely at the skeletons of reptiles that have two legs, or no legs, you can see they have bones that are like little leg stumps. These bones aren't legs now, but scientists believe they were legs in these animals, very long ago.

It seems that snakes, and birds with two legs, had ancestors that did have four legs! No one knows when or why these creatures gradually changed. Their great-great-great grandbabies are born with only two legs, or no legs today.

How this happened, when and why are some of the secrets of reptiles still to be discovered!

This is a crocodile. Look at his eye. He has a second eyelid that is see-through so he can close his eye underwater but still look around. Photo courtesy of Felix Broennimann via Pixabay.

Why do some reptiles eat stones?

Have you ever seen wild birds picking up very small stones and eating them? Did you wonder why?

Birds swallow little stones to grind up their food. Without the stones, they wouldn't be able to digest it.

Sea crocodiles also swallow stones. They do it to make themselves heavier. This helps them dive deeper in the ocean to find food.

Sea crocodiles are also called salt water crocodiles. They can grow to be 12 1/2 feet (3.8 m) long. The largest salt water crocodile ever found weighed 2,000 pounds (907 kg)!

This means this sea croc weighs about half as much as a car!

Are reptiles smart?

Animals are as smart as they need to be to survive and have babies, so their kind does not die out.

Some creatures have developed clever ways to do this.

One way is they've learned to hunt by tracking their prey. The only reptile known to do this is the komodo dragon.

It watches an animal it wants to eat, following it like a female lion.

The komodo can poison its prey, just enough to make it weak. Then the komodo follows the weakened prey until it's tired and easy to kill.

Komodo dragons mostly attack other animals, but they sometimes attack people.

When scientists wondered just how smart turtles are, they decided to have a contest between wood turtles and white rats.

Rats are a mammal and the smartest rodent.

They put both these creatures in a maze. A maze is like a puzzle. You must find your way out of it. The scientists did this experiment many times.

Can you guess which creature found the path out the fastest every time?

It was the wood turtles!

This is a wild iguana from Mexico.

Can reptiles see in colour? Can they change their own colour?

Many creatures can see in colour.

This doesn't mean they see in colour the same way people do.

Some lizards do see most colours, except red.

But they can see at night or when there is very little light, something people can't do nearly as well.

Some can also see types of light humans can't see. This helps them find their food.

This is a chameleon. They can change the colour of their entire bodies.

Many creatures change their body colours or patterns. Often, babies look different than adults.

Baby gecko lizards have spots that turn into spots and stripes on the adults.

Tuataras' colours change as they get older.

Most birds are dull colours as babies and don't develop their brighter colours until they're adults.

Male cardinals become bright red in mating season to attract a mate and have babies. At other times of the year, they are a duller or pale red.

The male bee hummingbird's head turns red to attract a mate.

In the bird world, the males are almost always more colourful than the females.

Chameleon lizards change colour when they are angry or stressed.

Some change colour to match the branch or soil they are standing on.

There are many creatures who use their colour to blend in with where they are, hoping their enemies won't see them.

This includes most types of snakes and lizards. Their camouflage colour gives you a good clue about where they live.

Most ground snakes are brown. Most lizards that spend their lives in trees are green.

What If You Could Change Colour What Colour Would You Be?

Bright red? Orange? Pink?

Or maybe purple?

If you were an Anole or a Chameleon, you might be able to change to any of these colours, any time you wanted to.

How cool would that be?

These are blue and yellow macaws.

Do reptiles live longer than people?

Generally, wild animals do not live as long as they could in zoos or as pets.

Green iguanas live in Mexico and the countries of Central America and South America. They usually live about 12 years or so. But in a zoo or as a pet they can live up to 20 years.

A ball python snake can live twice as long, or 40 years. Alligators can live for 70 years, almost as long as most people live. Pet parrots can live for 150 years, with good care!

But this still isn't the record-holder for the Longest-Living Reptile. The winner in this contest is the Galapagos giant tortoise. They can live for 190 years!

Some reptiles can toss their tails!

Some reptiles use a very odd way to escape when they're caught by an enemy.

They let their tails fall off! Some types of geckos, skinks and some other lizards do this. The tail wiggles to confuse the enemy, while the lizard without a tail escapes.

The tail will grow back, but it will be a little stumpy tail and not as colourful as the original tail.

Why don't reptiles chew their food?

Reptiles can't chew their food. Their jaws don't work the way mammals' jaws do.

Some reptiles, like geckos, can only eat food that's small enough to swallow whole. They must bite and tear their food. They can't chew it into small pieces before swallowing.

Snakes are different. A garter snake can swallow a mouse or frog that is twice as big as the snake's head! A snake can digest the whole creature it swallowed, bones and all!

Swallowing their prey whole wouldn't be possible if snakes didn't have a flexible skull. This skull is made up of many bones. They can make their jaws bigger, something no other creature can do.

This is a worm lizard. Photo by Richard Avery.

Is it a worm? Is it a snake? No – it's a lizard!

This lizard has no legs!

Most people think that snakes are the only reptile that must slither or creep because it has no legs. This isn't true!

There's one type of lizard that has no legs. It's the worm lizard and it lives in Spain. Though it looks just like a large blue worm, when you look closely it has eyelids. It also has ears you can see.

Worm lizards can close their eyes and they can hear, something no snake can do.

This is a broadhead skink. Wild skinks are a useful animal to have in the garden because they eat cockroaches, earwigs, slugs and other insects that might eat your plants. Photo by Dennis Giardina.

Are reptiles good parents?

Most reptiles aren't very good parents. They lay their eggs and leave, so their babies must rely on instinct for survival from the moment they hatch. Instinct is everything you already know how to do when you're born.

Some birds are excellent parents, feeding their babies until they are ready to leave the nest. Once the babies are out of the nest, the parents teach them how to find food and shelter. Some birds, like crows, live in family groups. Older sisters help care for the new chicks.

Most reptiles prefer to live alone for most of the time, except when they're looking for a mate.

This is a garter snake.

Do reptiles hibernate?

Hibernate means sleep through winter or until there's more water and food available. Many mammals and some reptiles hibernate.

In places where winter is cold or where summer is too hot, skinks burrow into the ground to protect themselves. They hibernate until spring.

As autumn weather becomes colder, garter snakes gather in stone dens underground. There could be hundreds, or even thousands, of snakes in these dens, sleeping through the winter.

As the weather warms up, the snakes wake up.

In spring, the males come up from the dens first and wait for the females to follow them. They mate, then all the snakes scatter, to find their own hunting grounds.

Bearded dragons are one of the few land reptiles that can swim. This pet beardie is playing in a swimming pool.

This sea snake is swimming past some coral.

Can reptiles swim?

Most reptiles live on land and aren't good swimmers.

One exception is sea snakes. They spend all their lives in water.

All the animals in the crocodile family can swim and spend most of their time in the water. They must return to land to lay their eggs.

Bearded dragons are one of the other reptiles that can swim, but only do it if they must. Sometimes bearded dragons and geckos will look for shallow water to get into because it helps them shed their skin.

Like snakes, their skin doesn't stretch. They must shed it every time they're ready to grow bigger.

33

This is a wild Cape Dwarf Chameleon. It lives in South Africa. Photo by Ross Dismore.

MORE ABOUT LIZARDS

Lots of people just love lizards – and there are lotsa lizards to love.

Scientists have found and described more than 6,000 types of lizards. They know there are probably even more we don't know about yet.

Some live in the desert. Others call the rainforests their homes. And some types of lizards are happy to live with people as pets.

The most popular lizards to have as pets are also the ones that are friendliest and easiest to care for. They are Bearded Dragons and Leopard Geckos.

This is a Mexican mole lizard.

Is this a lizard or a worm?

If you find this creature, you might think it looks just like a worm. It's not, because it's a lizard.

There are about 180 types of Worm Lizards. Many are pink, but some are other colours, including blue.

All are very skinny. Almost all are 6 inches (150 mm) long or less.

Worm lizards have sharp teeth. They hunt in tunnels made by leafcutter ants to find the beetle larvae they like to eat.

Worm Lizards' eyes are covered with skin and scales, so they can't see very well. They can tell the difference between light and dark, but probably can't see more than blurry shapes.

Another strange thing about Worm Lizards is the way they move. They have very loose skin and squeeze it and then expand like an accordion. They can do this going forward or backwards.

This is a model of what a Psittacosaurus dinosaur might have looked like.

Dinosaurs And Lizards – What's The Difference?

The word Dinosaur means "terrible lizard." They got this name almost 200 years ago when dinosaur fossils were first discovered and studied by scientists.

All the dinosaurs became extinct about 65 million years ago.

Today, scientists know that dinosaurs and lizards are two very different animals.

Modern lizards have four short legs that attach to the sides of their bodies.

Dinosaurs had longer legs that allowed them to stand upright.

Dinosaurs also had teeth with roots into their jaws, like people do today.

Lizards have rows of teeth that sit in grooves along their jaws.

Lizards are cold-blooded.

For many years, most scientists believed that dinosaurs were also cold-blooded. But new discoveries are showing that dinosaurs weren't cold-blooded, like lizards.

They also weren't warm-blooded, like birds and mammals. It seems that dinosaurs were something in between. Exactly what remains a mystery scientists are eager to solve.

Even with all these differences, there are some modern lizards that look a lot like some ancient dinosaurs.

One dinosaur that looks like it might be a lizard is Psittacosaurus. Here's how to say it: SIT-a-coe-sore-rus. It's a dinosaur that lived in China about 120 million years ago.

Scientists have recently discovered that Psittacosaurus was mainly brown, but had a paler belly, a dark face and a beak like a parrot.

Psittacosaurus was about as big as a Labrador Retriever dog.

It had a face that looked something like a chicken. It could run on it's hind legs.

Lizards Aren't Poisonous To Humans

There are two types of lizards that use poison to protect themselves when they're attacked. These two are Gila Monsters and Mexican Bearded Lizards.

If a Gila Monster or Mexican Bearded Lizard bit you, that bite would hurt. You'd be sick for a while, but you'd get better.

It's very rare for a human to be bitten by one of these lizards.

Some people think that some lizards have a stinger in their tails, but this is not true. There is no lizard that uses its tail to sting.

Some Humans Are Dangerous For Lizards

Would you be surprised if you went to your favourite restaurant and there was lizard on the menu? Maybe you'd order a lizard burger, or lizard fingers, or even lizard ice cream...?

That probably won't happen. But in some places in the world, people do eat lizards.

In the countries of Central America, Green Iguanas are a popular dish. Some people even call iguanas the "chicken of the tree." All iguanas like to climb trees and people who eat them say they taste like chicken.

In Africa, some people call Desert Lizards the "fish of the desert," and say they're delicious!

This tortoise is just hatching.

Lizards Lay Eggs

Each little lizard starts life in its own egg. But instead of that egg being a hard shell, like bird eggs, a lizard egg is more like a leather sack.

Like some birds, baby lizards have a special tool for breaking out of their egg. This tool is called an egg tooth. After they hatch, they lose their egg tooth.

Almost all mother lizards leave their eggs to hatch on their own. The babies have to fend for themselves from the moment they are born!

Only a few types of lizards stay and defend their eggs from enemies that might try to eat the eggs. Two of these good-parent lizards are Skinks and Glass Lizards.

This is a leopard gecko. Photo by Elvis Santana.

Wave To Your Lizard!

Only one type of lizard has a voice. It's the Leopard Gecko. They hiss or squeal when they're upset.

All the other types of lizards are silent. But they can communicate with each other or a predator by using body language.

Body language is saying something with your face or your body, not with words. When you smile, nod your head for "yes" or do a thumbs-up or a high-five you're using body language.

If you have a pet Bearded Dragon, you might have seen them bobbing their head, or waving with their front foot. That's lizard body language.

Have You Ever Seen A Lizard Make Itself BIG?

One of the ways some lizards scare their enemies is to make themselves look fierce. They might fill their lungs with air to look bigger. Or puff up the spiky skin under their mouth.

This is what a Bearded Dragon does and how they got their name. When they're attacked, their 'beard' will appear. It isn't really a beard, just the scaly skin under their chin.

Sometimes this skin will turn a darker colour when the Bearded Dragon feels threatened. It's meant to scare off an attacker.

Pet Bearded Dragons sometimes show their beards when they're upset.

Some Anoles can also do this by puffing up a sac of skin under their chin.

Show Us All Your Teeth!

Most lizards are constantly losing their teeth and growing in new ones. The only time people can do this is when we lose baby teeth and get our adult teeth. For most people this happens when they are about 8 years old.

But lizards keep getting new teeth over and over for their whole lives.

This is a horned lizard.

Lizard Horror Show!

The Horned Lizard is also called a Horned Toad because it looks more like a toad than like a lizard. But it's a lizard.

And one with a creepy ability. Horned Lizards can spurt blood from a horn next to their eyes. They do this to scare off their enemies.

An odd thing is they only do blood spurting when they're caught by a mammal, not when their enemy is another lizard.

Speed-Demon Lizards!

Many lizards can run. Some can even run going backwards.

There are some geckos that can run upside down and backwards at the same time!

The fastest lizard racer is the 6-Lined Racerunner. Its land-race record is 18 miles per hour (or 29 kilometers per hour).

If you had a race and the racers were a horse, a greyhound dog, a hummingbird, a racerunner lizard and Usain Bolt, who is the fastest human runner in the world, who do you think would win?

Do you think it would be the lizard?

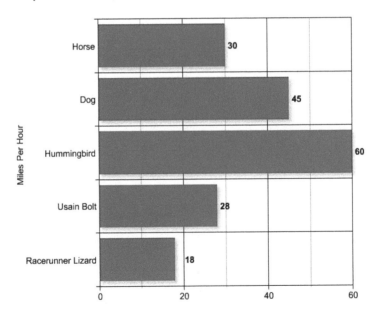

So, in our race, a bird would win. The lizard would come in last!

What Does Air Taste Like?

The reason that lizards have a very good sense of smell is they can taste the air.

This tells them when a friend or predator is near. It also helps them find food.

Lizards and snakes are the two types of reptiles that taste the air. That's what they're doing when they stick their tongues out.

Here's another thing snakes and lizards both do. They shed their skin. This is so they can grow larger.

When their skin is getting too tight, it breaks and comes off.

This can be in one big piece, or in little bits. Losing their skin like this is called molting. They need water to help them shed the old skin.

When these animals are babies or still young, they shed their skin more often than when they're adults. This is because very young animals grow quickly. They stop growing as adults.

Really Hungry Lizards

All lizards are good eaters. Some eat mainly plants. Some eat mostly insects. A few eat both plants and other animals.

A Thorny Devil Lizard can eat as many as 45 ants in just one minute!

Lizards Are Cold-blooded

Just like all reptiles except birds, lizards are cold-blooded. This means their own bodies can't use their stored energy to warm them up or cool them down.

Warm-blooded animals store energy as fat on their bodies.

This is so they can use the fat when they can't find food.

Wild cold-blooded creatures must have sun for heat. They need shady places to go to when they get too hot.

When a cold-blooded creature is a pet, they must have both a warm place and a cooler area in their tank.

Birds and mammals are warm-blooded. When mammals are too hot, they sweat to cool off.

When they're cold, their bodies can turn their stored fat into heat.

One Odd Thing About Lizard Scales

Like snakes and all other reptiles, lizards have scales. But lizards have more scales on their bellies than on their backs!

This little reptile can spread its wings to glide between the trees, which is why it's called the Flying Lizard. They live in tropical rainforests in Southeast Asia.

Flying Lizards

Tiny Flying Dragon Lizards don't have wings and they can't fly.

What they do have is even more amazing. It's skin they can spread out like a cape, allowing them to glide between trees.

When they aren't gliding, their capes fold flat against their bodies and they look like other lizards, with four legs.

Flying Lizards live in the forests of South East Asia.

This is a green mamba snake. Photo courtesy of Rabe on Pixabay.

MORE ABOUT SNAKES

Snakes can live almost everywhere in the world. This includes lakes, oceans, streams and forests. Also in deserts, on the ground, underground and in trees. There are almost 3,000 different snake species. About 500 of these types of snakes are poisonous. Of these, only about 40 are poisonous to humans.

The most dangerous place in the world to be, if you're worried about poisonous snakes, is Australia. There are more venomous (this means poison) snakes in Australia than non-venomous (not poison) snakes. A snake's own poison can't kill it.

Snakes all have long, strong and flexible bodies. This helps them move very quickly when they want to, even though they don't have legs.

This snake was born with two heads. Photo by Vieleineinerhuelle on Pixabay

If you looked at a snake skeleton, you would see it has a backbone and a lot of ribs. A snake can have as many as 400 ribs. People have 24 ribs.

Snakes can use their strong muscles to move forward, backward or sideways. Some can slide forward on the ground. They are 'walking' on their ribs and scales.

Other snakes slither forward and sideways, pushing against the ground with their muscles to move.

Sometimes, creatures are born with some very odd mistakes. One of these mistakes that can happen with snakes is they can have two heads! If a snake is born with two heads, the two heads will try to fight with each other.

This is the black mamba snake.

What are the world's most dangerous snakes?

Most snakes are shy. They'd much rather escape than bite!

Deaths by snake bite are rare everywhere in the world except for one country. That country is India.

Many thousands of people die in India each year after being bitten by a Saw-Scaled Carpet Viper. They could have lived if they got the anti-venom medicine right away.

If you are travelling in a country that has poisonous snakes, you must take anti-venom with you and know how to use it.

If you saw a black mamba, you might wonder about the name of this snake, because its skin is dark greenish-gray.

But if you were near a black mamba when it showed the part of its body that is black, you'd be in terrible danger. You'd need to get the anti-venom medicine right away.

When a black mamba opens its black mouth wide, hisses and sticks out its long black tongue, it's about to attack!

They strike and bite not just once, but many times.

A person who is bitten by a black mamba and doesn't have any anti-venom medicine with them will die in about 20 minutes.

Don't think you would be able to just run away. Black mambas can slither at 12.5 miles per hour (or 20 km per hour).

Some athletes can run this fast. Most people can't without a lot of training.

Black Mambas are the longest poisonous snakes in Africa, growing to be 14 feet (4.5 m) long.

Another dangerous land snake is the Inland Taipan.

It lives in parts of Australia. One bite has enough venom to kill 100 people, or 250,000 mice! But strangely enough, as far as we know, no human has ever been killed by this snake in modern times.

All Sea Snakes Are Poisonous!

Most of the 70 species of sea snakes live in the warmest parts of the Pacific Ocean and in the Indian Ocean. They like to live in shallow water, especially near coral reefs.

All sea snakes have a flat tail that helps them swim. They also can close their nostrils (that's the nose opening) when they're underwater.

Sea snakes have big lungs, so they can stay underwater a long time. They can also 'breath' through their skin, getting oxygen from the water through their skin.

Some snakes can stay underwater for two hours before they need to come back to the surface to breath!

All sea snakes have venom that's poisonous. Snake venom works by paralyzing the snake's prey. Usually, sea snakes use their venom on fish, but it can be dangerous for humans.

A Beaked Sea Snake has enough venom to kill 50 people in one bite.

Scientists are investigating how to use certain snake venoms for new medicines to cure diseases.

It could be that one day, we will be able to cure cancer or other serious illnesses using a medicine made from snake venom.

These gharials live in a zoo. Photo by Maky Orel via Pixabay.

MORE ABOUT CROCODILIANS

The Crocodilians are the family of creatures including Crocodiles, Alligators, Caimans and Gharials. Most crocodilians live in tropical places.

They all look pretty much the same, with a long body, four legs and a lot of sharp teeth.

The gharials have long, pointy snouts. The caimans are the smallest, getting to be about 5 feet (1.5 metres) long. The largest are the ocean crocodiles.

All crocodilians use their powerful jaws to capture and crush their prey. They eat fish, frogs, turtles and birds. They will also attack animals like dogs or cats and can hurt or kill people.

One strange thing they do is close their throat when they're underwater.

No water gets to their lungs or stomach when they attack underwater.

Some live in muddy water, where it's hard to see. Instead, they sense where their prey is with sensors in their skin that can feel changes in water pressure.

Pressure means how hard something is pressing against something else.

Ever tasted a crocodile burger?

In some parts of the world, people eat reptiles! Snake, crocodile and alligator meat and eggs are considered delicacies.

There are birds that you've probably eaten many times – chickens and turkeys.

And there are other ways people benefit from reptiles besides eating some of them.

The hides (that's the skins) of Australian crocodiles are used to make handbags, shoes, boots, belts and wallets.

And scientists use some of these animals for their research.

Good mother alligator

Except for birds, most reptiles aren't very good parents. They leave before their babies ever get to know them or learn from them.

All the crocodilians lay eggs, generally once a year.

The American Alligator lives in swamps, lakes and rivers in several American states from North Carolina to Texas and Florida.

It builds a nest of mud, leaves and sticks and then stays near the nest for eight weeks to scare off predators.

Then the eggs hatch. The tiny baby alligators call out to their mother. She picks them up and carries them to the water. They will stay with their mother until they are one year old.

Alligator Brain Freeze!

What happens if an alligator's warm lake, river or swamp suddenly gets very cold in winter?

Some alligators that live in North America and China have learned to adapt. *Adapt* means change to survive. They can do this even if their lake or river freezes over. They can leave their head frozen in the ice at the surface, with just their nose sticking out to breath.

They can survive this way for several months, something no other creature can do!

These beautiful birds are macaws. Macaws live in Mexico and the countries of Central America and South America. Most of them live in the rainforests.

MORE ABOUT BIRDS

Experts don't agree about if birds should belong in the reptile family, or in their own family.

Here's why. All reptiles are cold-blooded, but birds and mammals are warm-blooded.

No reptile can fly, but most birds can. Part of what makes flight possible for some birds is that their bones

This bird is called a kingfisher. Photo courtesy of Timo Schluter on Pixabay.

are strong but hollow. This is why birds weigh less than mammals or reptiles of the same size.

The wing of a bird has the same bones as a human arm. It's just that these bones are arranged a bit differently.

Why would scientists put birds in the reptile family?

It's because the closest living creature to birds is crocodiles. This might seem hard to believe, but it's true.

Birds and crocodiles are the closest living creatures to some ancient dinosaurs. Not in the way they look, but because of the ways their bodies work.

What do you think?

Should birds be in the reptile family? Or should they be in their own group?

Are parrots smart enough to learn how to talk?

Parrots are excellent mimics, which means they can copy the sound of a word they hear. But they don't know what that word means. If they make that sound and someone gives them a treat, they will keep doing it.

Penguins can't fly. Why are they birds?

Penguins live in the coldest places in the Southern Hemisphere, mostly in Antarctica. There are no penguins in the Far North and Arctic.

They're a bird, but they can't fly. They spend about half their time on land and the rest of their time in the water, hunting for the fish they eat.

Like all birds, penguins are warm-blooded. They lay just one egg and then protect it until it hatches. On land, their strong tails help them walk upright, the same way people walk.

In the water, they tuck their feet back against their tail and use their arms like flippers, the same as sea turtles do.

Some other types of birds that can't fly are ostriches, emus, cassowaries, rheas and kiwis. They are all too heavy and their wings are too weak for them to be able to fly.

This is a sea turtle swimming past coral. Turtles are slow-moving and awkward on land, but as graceful as flying birds in the water. Photo by Skeeze on Pixabay.

MORE ABOUT TURTLES & TORTOISES

Turtles and tortoises live almost everywhere there is water, including lakes, swamps, rivers and in the ocean. Some like to live mostly on land. Tortoises live entirely on land.

Their shells are made of separate bones that join together. Hard scales or leathery skin covers their bony shells. Their shells are attached to their skeletons. Turtles cannot leave their shells.

Most turtles and tortoises can pull their head and legs into their shell to protect themselves. Some, like box turtles, can climb completely into their shell. Sea turtles can't do this.

Female sea turtles only return to land every two or three years. They always go back to the beach where they were born to make a nest and lay 60 to 160 eggs. Then they hurry back to the ocean.

Warmed by the sun, the eggs hatch. The baby turtles make a dash for the sea, but few of them make it.

Out of every 200 sea turtle eggs, only 2 baby turtles will live long enough to become adults. This is one of the reasons that they are threatened or endangered in many places in the world.

Other reasons are that some people hunt and eat turtles, they have lost their nesting beaches when people build big hotels there, or they get caught in fishing nets.

Turtles are very slow-moving and clumsy on land, but strong and graceful swimmers in the ocean. They look like they're flying through the water!

Sea turtles migrate between their feeding and nesting places.

Each year, they can travel many hundreds of miles (or more than 1,000 km), even crossing entire oceans!

This is a sea turtle.

What's the difference between a turtle and a tortoise?

Tortoises can't swim. They live entirely on land and eat only plants. Turtles swim, some of them living in the water almost all their lives. They eat plants and other creatures, like insects, fish and frogs.

Tortoises stay with their eggs and protect their babies until they are about 80 days old. Turtles lay their eggs and leave. Baby turtles are born knowing how to survive.

Tortoises have a dome-shaped shell. Turtles have a shell that is flatter, or rounded, helping them move better in the water.

Both have a hard, bony shell and long claws on their feet.

Boy Turtles or Girl Turtles?

Here's an odd thing about turtles. The temperature of the eggs in their nest is what tells if the little turtles will be males or females.

If the sand or their nest is warmer, most or all the baby turtles will be females.

If it's cooler, most will be males. And if the temperature is in the middle, some will be boys and some will be girls.

And here's another very odd reptile fact. If the eggs in a nest are crocodile eggs, a warmer nest means most of the babies will be males. A cooler nest means most of the babies will be female crocodiles.

Do turtles have ears?

Turtles and snakes have no outer ear. An outer ear is an ear you can see on the outside of their heads.

But they do have inner ears, the part of the ear inside the head connected to the brain. They can't hear sounds, but they can sense vibrations in the earth.

Vibration is the sound that happens when something moves. Imagine that you pound a drum, but you don't hear the drum beat. If you touch the drum right after you hit it, you can feel the drum moving. What you are feeling is the vibration.

This is a tuatara from New Zealand.

MORE ABOUT THE TUATARA

What is the world's rarest reptile?

Tuataras are the world's rarest reptiles. Here's how to say their name: too-a-tara-a. There is only one type alive in the world today.

Once there were many types, but now all the others are extinct. The one species of tuatara that survives lives only on remote islands off the New Zealand shore. Tuataras are endangered, meaning they could become extinct unless we help them and protect their homes.

Wild tuataras are seldom seen by people. But if you did see one, here's what it would look like. It's a small creature, with olive green or brownish or orangey-red skin. It has a head that looks something like a turtle.

The males, who are bigger than the females, can grow to be almost 20 inches (.5 metre) long and weight as much as just a bit more than 3 pounds (1.5 kg). Males have spines on the top of their heads and along their backbone.

One odd thing about tuataras is that they only need to breathe once every hour.

How does this compare to how fast people breathe?

Right now, when you are reading, you breathe about 20 times a minute, or 1,200 times in an hour.

If you were running or swimming, you'd be breathing much faster.

Another odd thing is how long this little lizard lives. Their biggest enemy is rats, who eat their eggs. Today, all tuataras live on islands where there are no rats.

They can live for about 60 years, though some can get to be up to 100 years old! That's a very long life, for a lizard!

Here's what humans are doing to help the tuataras survive in New Zealand. They're making sure no rats ever get to the islands where the tuataras live.

They're also taking some tuataras to other remote islands where there are no other creatures except birds, hoping that the tuataras will make this their safe new home.

This is a corn snake. They are very common pets for people who like reptiles.

Do reptiles make good pets?

Though their lives are often difficult and short, most wild creatures would much rather have their wild, natural lives than live in a zoo or be a pet.

The only animal on earth that chooses to live with people as a pet and is much happier as a pet, is the cat.

All animals (except, possibly, some cats) have a strong need to be outside and roam through their territory. Territory is all the land that they consider to be theirs, sort of like your home is your territory.

They also have a strong instinct to have babies, which might not happen if they are a pet or in a zoo.

Being in a cage, tank or bowl may cause them so much stress that they get sick or they die.

But there are a few reptiles that can be content as pets if they get good care and enough attention.

Reptiles are not the easiest pets to have. If you or your family have never had a pet before, you probably shouldn't choose a reptile as your first pet.

The best reptile pets don't hurt people, are interesting and are somewhat easy to care for. They are:

1. Bearded dragons

2. Leopard geckos

3. Ball python snakes

4. Corn snakes

5. Parakeets or Budgies

If you decide to have a reptile pet, you must always wash your hands carefully with soap and hot water before you touch them and right after you touch them.

This is to keep both you and your pet healthy. There are some illnesses that pets can catch from people or that people can catch from pets. Remembering to wash your hands protects you and your pet!

This little green lizard is wild but protected. It lives in an animal sanctuary park in Asia.

Are reptiles endangered?

Our world is changing rapidly in ways that aren't healthy for animals. Most of these changes aren't caused by nature; they are caused by people.

These changes are making it harder for many creatures, including reptiles, to survive. There are already some animals that used to live on earth, but now they do not. The last one has died. They are gone forever. They are extinct.

There are more that could vanish in your lifetime. One of these is the Tuatara.

Another are the Kemp's Ridley Sea Turtles. They're the world's most endangered species of sea turtle. Endangered means that there aren't very many left. Sadly, today many animals are on the Endangered List.

Kemp's Ridley sea turtle females always come back to the same beach where they were born to lay their eggs.

Until just a few years ago there was only one beach where Kemp's Ridley turtles laid their eggs. This one beach is at Tamaulipas, in northeast Mexico. But this beach has become so popular with tourists that it is even more dangerous for the turtles.

When people need the land, animals usually lose out.

But some people in Mexico and in United States are working hard to save the Kemp's Ridley turtles. They watch the nests and take the new babies as soon

This is a Kemp's Ridley sea turtle.

as they hatch. This is when baby turtles must run to the ocean and safety. But there are many shore birds waiting to eat them before they get there.

Instead, scientists collect new baby turtles as soon as they hatch. They put these baby Kemp's Ridley turtles in tanks and look after them until they're big enough to be able to defend themselves. Then they are released at the beach that is their new home on South Padre Island, Texas. They help them get safely to the ocean.

As adults, some of the females will return to this protected beach in Texas each year to lay their eggs.

This could mean that the Kemp's Ridley sea turtle, which is endangered today, might survive.

Humans are causing all these problems, or allowing them to happen

All the creatures on earth are depending on humans to save them from many threats. These threats include pollution, garbage in the oceans, the fishing industry and climate change. What can you do to help?

You've already started, by being interested in these creatures and learning more about them.

You can continue to learn more about the animals we share our world with at school, at the library or by volunteering to help wildlife.

There are many organizations that always need help from people who care about animals and our planet. Here are just some of the ways they do this. They:

- Clean litter out of rivers to help the fish, frogs and turtles.
- Build bridges or tunnels, so animals won't be hit by cars when they're trying to cross the road.
- Work to save endangered habitats like the islands where tuataras live or where turtles lay their eggs. *Habitats* means their homes.
- Help educate other people about how important it is to save the animals.

What will <u>you</u> do to make a difference?

How can you help the animals?

This green iguana is having fun.

Thank you!

I hope you've enjoyed reading this book of strange and amazing facts about all the creatures in the reptile family, including lizards, crocodilians, birds, snakes, turtles and tortoises and the tuatara.

If you want to know more about the world's most fascinating and fantastic creatures, including some that make great pets, keep reading!

Best wishes,

Jacquelyn

About Jacquelyn

Jacquelyn Elnor Johnson writes books about pets for children. Her family has just one pet, a cat named Boots. But in the past, there have been many wonderful dogs in her life, including Dachshunds, Poodles and a black Labrador Retriever.

She and her family live in Nova Scotia, Canada.

More fun pet and animal books you might like, all written for kids who are 9 to 12, or in grades three to seven:

Best Pets for Kids Series:

> I Want a Puppy
>
> I Want a Kitten
>
> I Want a Bearded Dragon
>
> I Want a Leopard Gecko

Fun Pets for Kids Series:

> Small Fun Pets; Beginner Pets for Kids 9-12
>
> Top 10 Fun Pets for Kids 9-12

Fun Animal Facts for Kids Series:

> Fun Dog Facts for Kids 9-12
>
> Fun Cat Facts for Kids 9-12
>
> Fun Leopard Gecko and Bearded Dragon Facts for Kids 9-12
>
> Fun Reptile Facts for Kids 9-12; Lizards, Turtles, Crocodilians, Snakes and Birds

CPSIA information can be obtained
at www.ICGtesting.com
Printed in the USA
LVHW072352090122
708167LV00001B/4